Kids' Letters From Camp

Compiled and Edited by Bill Adler

A Birch Lane Press Book
Published by Carol Publishing Group

A Birch Lane Press Book
Published by Carol Publishing Group

Birch Lane Press is a registered trademark of Carol Communications, Inc.
Editorial Offices: 600 Madison Avenue, New York, N.Y. 10022
Sales and Distribution Offices: 120 Enterprise Avenue, Secaucus, N.J. 07094
In Canada: Canadian Manda Group, P.O. Box, Station U, Toronto, Ontario M8Z 5P9
Queries regarding rights and permissions should be addressed to Carol Publishing Group,
600 Madison Avenue, New York, N.Y. 10022

Carol Publishing Group books are available at special discounts for bulk purchases, sales promotions, fund-raising, or educational purposes. Special editions can be created to specifications. For details, contact Special Sales Department, Carol Publishing Group, 120 Enterprise Avenue, Secaucus, N.J. 07094

Design by Steven Brower and Diane Y. Chin

Manufactured in the United States of America

10 9 8 7 6 5 4 3 2 1

Library of Congress Cataloging-in-Publication Data

Kids' letters from Camp / Compiled and Edited by Bill Adler.
            p. cm.
            "A Birch Lane Press Book."
            ISBN 1-55972-226-6
            1. Camps—United States—Humor.
            2. Children—United States—Correspondence. I. Adler, Bill
            GV193.K53 1994
            796.54'2'0207—dc20   93-46693
                                           CIP

Dear Mother and Dad:

Thank you for sending me the clothes but I really need food.
They give you nothing to eat here exept bread and water and cheerios.

Love
Jonathan
Suarez

By Jonathan
Suarez

3

Dear Mom and Dad,

This camp isn't at all like the pictures in the book that the man showed us when he came to our house!

Your daughter
Caroline

Dear Pop:

Our team won the baseball championship because the other team didn't show up. They had poison ivy.

Love,
Rachael L.

Dear Mother and Dad

Camp is nice but it isn't as much fun as Disneyland.

Love
Eddie
Joe
Old Tappan

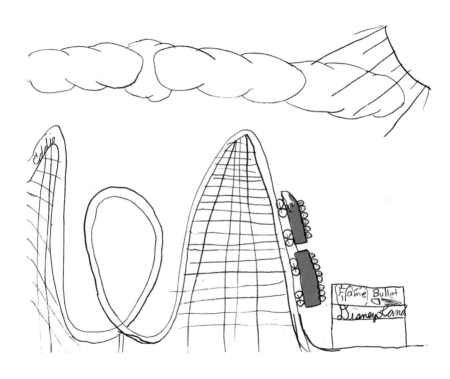

Dear Mother and Father,
    How can I have any fun here?
There isn't any T.V. here.

                Your homesick daughter,
                    Emily

Dear Grandpa,
   I want to write to you and tell you all the nice
things about camp but you told me never to lie.
                    your grandaughter,
                         Jessica L.

Dear Mother,

Please send me a case of ketchup. All the kids put ketchup on everything. That's the only way we can eat the food.

Love
Jessi

Dear Mom

All the kids in the bunk got sick except for Michael. Michael is going to be a doctor when he grows up.

Love
Linda
6

Dear dad:
Please send me my allowance.
I want to buy a new ~~new~~ counselor.

From Simon

Dear Mom:
I can't write home everyday. Please read the letter I wrote yesterday again.

Love,
Kevin

DEAR FOLKS:
THE BEST
TIME AT CAMP
IS WHEN WE
SLEEP.

YOUR DAUGHTER

LIA

LIA

Dear Mother,

Everybody says that the cook at camp was a cook at prison before he came here.

Your starving daughter,
Emily Earl

Dear mom and dad:
we found a skunk in
our bunk. His name is
Larry
     xxx ooo Love
Rachel

Dear Bro,

I will write to you about all the things I like about this camp as soon as I think of one.

Your sister,
Tara

Tara
Age 10

Dear Mother and Dad,

I am bringing home a pet from camp. But don't worry. Snakes don't take up much room.

Your son
Phil

Dear Mom and Dad,

I'm having a good time at camp. I saw lots of animals and bugs. Some of the animals and bugs are snakes, turtles, fox, tigers, eagle, tarantula, mice! And I brought them home!!! And lots more!

See you!

Janna
Age 8
New Jersey

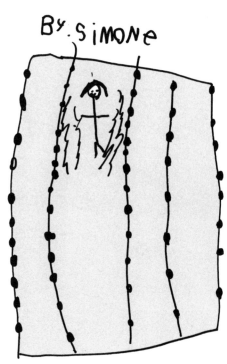

By SiMONE

DEAR. BENLIE.
HERe. IS. A. PICTURe

. OF. Me. SWIMMI Ne
. YOU. CANT. see. me.

TOO. GOOD. beCAUSe.
i. AM. UNDER. WATER. Se
YOU A. FRieND.
SiMONe

DEAR MOM AND DAD,
        TUESDAY I WENT OUT ON
THE LAKE IN A ROW BOAT. I
WAS THE ONLY KID THAT HAD A
ROW BOAT THAT DIDN'T LEAK.

                LOVE,
                    MARK

MARK

Dear grandma, and grandpa,
We are counting the days until
we leave camp and we are
free again.

love,
Sarah

Dear Grandpa and Grandma;
  I met a girl at the camp
dance. She is very pretty and
hates camp like me.

                    Your Grandson,
                    Andy

Dear MoM;
could you Please come up to camp To cook
for me.

Love,
Karrin

P.s. Even if you only make toast.

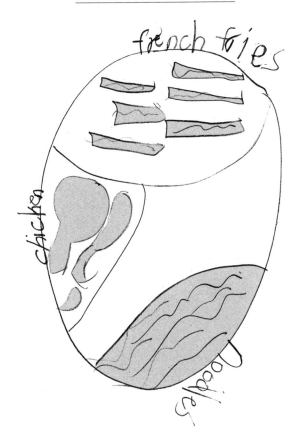

Dear: Dad and Mother

our bunk made a new name for
our camp we call it sing sing

Sam
age 9

Sam

43

Dear Mom and Dad:

Why did you send me to camp?
What did I do wrong?

Love
Ted

Dear Mom and Dad,
If you paid more than two cents
for this camp, you were gypped.

Love,
Bridget

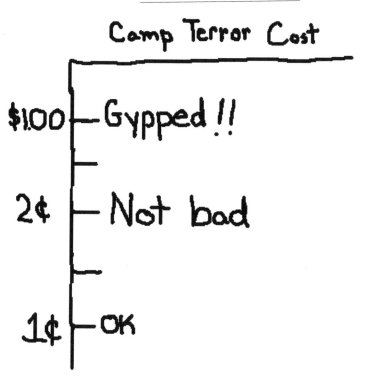

Bridget Fitzgerald
Age 10

47

Dear Mother and Dad,
  Dracula would love this camp.

        Your Son,

        Sebastian
        Age 8½,
        New York.

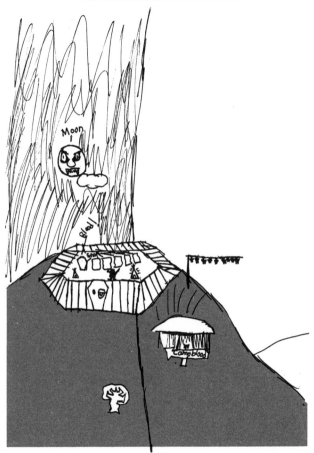

Dear Mother and Dad,

Somebody stole my tooth brush. I think I know who did it. It was the same kid who stole my toothpaste.

Love,
Bobby

DEAR MOM
EVERY WEEK AT
CAMP THEY MAKE
YOU TAKE A BATH
EVEN IF YOU DON'T
NEED ONE.

YOUR

DAUGHTER,

CARLA

Dear Mom,
the bugs bite
the food bite
everthing bites!!!!!
Love, Christina

Written and Drawn by Christina Romano

Dear Mother and Dad:
Please send me ~~two~~ left sneakers,
I have two right sneakers

Love
Paul

By Paul

Dear Folks:

All the kids in my bunk are slobs. I hope I have the same bunk again next summer.

Love,
Jessica Agelo

Dear Mom and Dad,
Everything at camp is okay and I am learning how to eat and put on my clothes with my left arm,

Your son,
John

John Fitzgerald
Age 8

Dear Mom and Dad

Could you send
my TV set to
camp

I am missing all
my favorite programs

Your Son
Jimmy

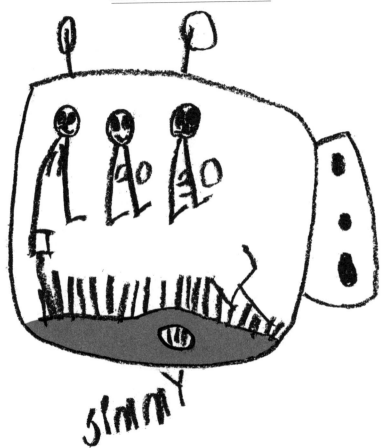

Jimmy

61

Dear Grandma and
Grandpa,
It rained every day at
camp this week and
all we could do is sleep in
our bed all day.

It was the best week
at camp.

Love
Samantha
6

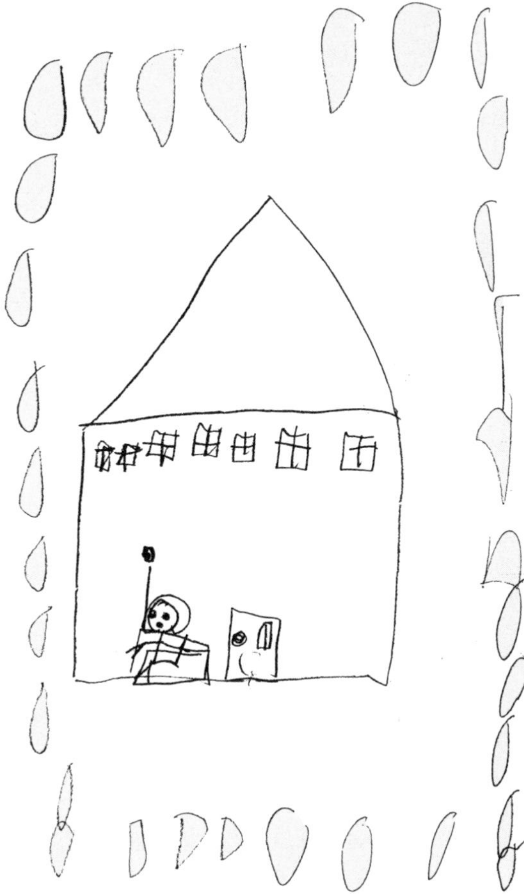

DEAR KIP
I HAVE ONLY ONE
REAL FRIEND AT CAMP
AND I DI HATE HIM O CAMP
YOUR
SISTER
MARISA
5

Special Thanks To:

Mark Abbate, Harry Black, Sebastian Black, Simone Breunig Balog, Emily Breunig, Drew Breunig, Lia Breunig, Janna Brower, Sam Campodonico-Ludwig, Simon Campodonico-Ludwig, Lara Dolan, Lisa Dolan, Emily Earl, Bridget Fitzgerald, John Fitzgerald, Sarah Hamilton, Jessica Harrington, Jimmy Hascup, Jessica Landress, Marisa Landress, Rachael Landress, Samantha Landress, Eddie Lewis, Kevin Lewis, Karrin Pitt, Christina Romano, Rachel Schragis, William Schragis, Jonathan Suarez.